Bluff

BLUFF

by

Adam Chiles

Measure Press
Savannah, Georgia

Printed in the United States of America
First Edition

The text of this book is composed in Baskerville.
Composition by R.G.
Manufacturing by Ingram.

Chiles, Adam
Bluff / by Adam Chiles — 1st ed.

ISBN-13: 978-1-939574-37-4
ISBN-10: 1-939574-37-4
Library of Congress Control Number: 2023945693

With thanks to Miriam Berkley for the author photo and Kristy Romeo for the cover art.

Measure Press
2 Longberry Lane
Savannah, GA 31419
http://www.measurepress.com/measure/

Acknowledgements

I am grateful to the editors of the following journals where some of these poems first appeared:

Allegro Poetry Review
Blackbird
Connotation Press
Cumberland River Review
Copper Nickel
The Cortland Review
Leveler
The Literary Review
Magma
The Malahat Review
The Moth
Nimrod International
OneArt
Permafrost
The Poetry Village
Prism International
Rhino
Salzburg Poetry Review
Terrain.org
Threepenny Review
Thrush Poetry Review
Whale Road Review
Willow Springs

There's the cloud's brumal attic was published as a part of the Thrush Poetry broadside series.

My Father's Hearing Aid was published by Broadsided Press as a broadside.

My gratitude to Rob Griffith, Paul Bone and all the fine folks at Measure Press for believing in this book and bringing it into the world. Also grateful acknowledgment to Kristy Romeo for her impeccable cover design which depicts the coastline of East Yorkshire, UK.

Massive thanks to T.R. Hummer, James Hoch, Dan O'Brien, Catherine Staples and Sidney Wade for lending the book their kind words.

Additional thanks to Catherine Staples for her careful reading of an early draft of *Bluff*.

A special thanks to James Hoch for his extensive advice on the manuscript.

Thanks also to Claudia Emerson my workshop mentor at the 2013 Sewanee Writers Conference for her boundless encouragement and careful reading of my work.

A hand clap, love and thanks to my son Noah who listened to me read many of these poems aloud again and again without complaint as I revised them!

Finally, my love, heart, and gratitude to my partner Emily, my first and last reader, for her invaluable editorial work and advice on multiple drafts. *Bluff* would not be what it is without her sharp ear and eyes. It's a privilege to walk this earth alongside you!

For my mother and father

CONTENTS

Spurn Point

We had neared the end of something
though it was morning, the day young.

Wind dragged at the marram grasses,
their green blades bending after the tide,

the draw of its waters hauling pebbles back,
reloading a depthless hull. And though

the light house had reopened as a museum,
something was receding in us, sat here

in the slow heat of the car, the peninsula,
newly breached. I could sense it —

this eclipse of sea and sky.
The tanker stalled on the horizon.

"A memory of the sea, it's what remains.
Homesickness in the rocks.
Homecoming in the trees."

— Li-Young Lee

Reading Edward Thomas to My Father

From the ninth-floor hospital window, acres broaden,
scroll out past slate and pylon, the black moor

unfastening, hour by hour, its thicket of wounds.
All afternoon, I give back willow-herb and grass,

the blackbird's carousel wing. I give back hunger, thirst,
lines that widened in him for almost a century,

widening again. I give back this catalogue of field
and sky, each word circling farther, farther in.

I give back haycock, pasture. Silence wheeling deeper.
I give back the ravening wing, the rapture.

Wreckage Song

Outside, the bird's soliloquy, a wreckage song
wrung from its furnace, steaming in the oak

like a charred vowel. It has already gone three.
Clocks unwind from gray mantels.

The sea drills closer. You can smell it —
these architectures of salt, these lashed abbreviations

tossing in land. Feel the northern cottages
flinch and stiffen under the gale.

Your oven tops switch on; a shiver of crowns.
The cat at your window is slinking out

of his animal night. You pace
behind the blinds, a bruised vernacular.

On the Platform of Paragon Station

Larkin swerves in trapped flight, face,
body, arrested in bronze, our godless
pedestrian star. Blocks away, sea gulls
shit above the quay as we slouch past,
heads bent, braced for the hour's scrim
of sleet, siren, cloud. And who wouldn't
shelter a spell under a city tree, or cafe
awning, hypnotized. Who wouldn't sense
here a chrism of desire as rain litters
the eye, a longing in us briefly awakened
before we press on, wedded to those
behind us, those ahead, winding home,
buttoned against the hail: worn paladins
of our nightly, weather-laden estates.

3 A.M.

the road is a ghost.
Believe it.

Beams push out
across the dale —

a Mini vanishing
into its own

pale arithmetic.

You dream of winter —
a minor road

a contusion sleeved
beyond the compass

of your bed.

Instructions for Water

I salve the tongue, lip, moistening
at intervals, sores beginning to crack
along the seam of his mouth. Three
days since he's been allowed water.
Periodically he lifts a hand and leans
forward as though holding a glass,
puts it to his lips and swallows
then rubs a finger against his throat;
nothing there, son, he seems to say,
a word loosening in him barely audible,
his tongue running along the dryness
of his lip. We're past forgiveness.
I ease the sponge into his mouth,
watch him suckle it as his fingers
curl again around the absent cup.
I follow my instructions, apply
the sponge at intervals. All morning
the sky spills through the 9th floor
window behind us, a remote
uninterrupted blue.

Bluff

A familiar script, the gull's
        attention to wind, white petal,
feather-slammed,

accustomed to bullying. Not me,
        I turn my back on it, claim
this pool room's lit pasture,

its geography of Bells, contemplate
        the erosions, a house inching
closer to the shore, another

toppled, gate open
        to cliff edge and horizon.
We're all headed for the bluff,

the gale, its clarifying salt.
        May as well enjoy the view,
I do. And when I step outside

for a smoke, night coming on,
        its final verse and chapter,
who knows what I become

rowing off, wind borne,
        my cigarette knitted to the dark,
all testimony pulled asunder.

Onion

My father sliced the onion in two,
and we sat, each lifting our half-moon.

He took a bite then another — as though
it was fruit — tasting the bald

sting of it, that temper of white flesh,
the car then full of heat, ozone.

And now a little stilton, he said,
smiling at me, doubling down

on the odor. The sea stretched out
in front of us. Afterwards, he dozed,

car windows slowly fogging
as I walked the edges of the cliff,

young still, the aftertaste of what
we'd eaten sharpening my breath.

After Visiting Hours

I drive home past the shuttered nurseries,
radio tuned to my father's station, wipers

sliding in and out of key. Think of him prone
on the ninth floor of Hull Royal Infirmary,

hands in restraint gloves so he can't drag out
the feeding tube. *Who am I,* I ask each visit

though he rarely answers, clots already
charting the lake inside — his body jailed,

fixed to the wires, the IV dripping like a clock.
Each night, I leave him this way, walk the stairs

down, indulging my fear of elevators, every step
a decompression as I fall back into the neon

circuitry of the city, thinking of him up there,
his eyes closing on the ceiling fan, the window

behind him, night in its infinite frame.

After the Call from the Night Nurse

4am, a steady agitation,
rain against glass. My father's

spring buds, bragging
fires through soil.

I lean back in his chair, listen.
Everything in the room

a kind of deafening. *Wheatfield*
with Crows, its migraine

latched above the mantel.
His books, records,

marshalled in their gilings.
The painted gourd pulsing,

a strange anatomy. These bifocals,
orphaned in my hand.

His oils, resins. I can smell him.
His chair a calendar of tar.

Call this pond a mirror, a stilled eye, the crow
its sculled iris. Dear cousin, you fly lawless

over these shallows, my tremolo, a black star
borne from hymnal lofts. Dear pioneer, you ink

the carp-lit surfaces, a felled cultic, hatching there.
Your unmoored shadow keys the evening waters.

The Afterlife

The night after my father died — not wanting to leave
my mother alone — I lugged a mattress into the room
and wedged it at the foot of her bed. All night, I lay there
listening to the neighbor's fountain spill its cold stanzas
into the iron grass, this room a kind of afterlife, an alcove
filled with the distant music of water. Each morning,
I'd prepare my mother's breakfast, a slice of dry toast,
a few grapes, a small glass of milk, then carry it back
to her where newly awake, her hair spread like a blanched
lake about her face and pillow, clarities of light pouring
into the room. Then downstairs, I'd take to my father's chair,
eyeing spring bully the still frozen surfaces of morning.
And later, switch on the snooker for my mother,
both of us silent in the familiar, stunned, embryonic air
of the living room, drifting along its verges, watching
as snooker balls fell routinely into the day's gray netting.

Nocturne

A wing stirred
in my mother now —
grief's unfolding
dialect. And who
knows which moor,
bracken-clad, was
fastening its pleat
of limestone inside.
Her ear trawled
the pillow's bedrock,
my father's voice
already thin. Already
a localized deafness,
a soundless ringing.

The Coroner's Waiting Room

A threadbare carpet greets my feet.
Gilt-edged portraits marshalling
the walls: old mayors in machineries
of office. Beyond, pre-war banisters
spiral skyward, the faint air of nicotine
still buried in stairwells, corridors.

Somewhere across town, a surgeon
studies the hemispheres lifted
from my father's body: was it the heart?
Or the way he lost his footing, the sill
of the door a blind spot as he stepped
away? I wait here. Now and then
a hinge closes a few flights above me.
Then silence again. Chancel-like.

Farm Track at Dusk

We pulled over a few miles from home,
cut the engine, rolled our windows down,
watched the bats one by one dip and lift
high above the cattle barns, the freshly
ploughed fields, woods, near silent now
under a failing September sky. By spring
you'd be gone. I thought of all the years
you'd ridden this back road without me,
this track I never knew existed, cutting
its way through farm, pasture, you, father,
driving its curves, its pocked soils home.
What shadows gripped us then: a combine's
distant harrowing, the skirl of wings aloft,
that darkness inking the herd steadily in.

Night Ride with My Mother

Our beams feed along the asphalt,
invite this carbon of flies. Trees

ache in their ashen chandeliers.
There's no strategy to this.

No compass out of the kingdom.
Hedges tangle like flayed umbrellas.

A barn owl ghosts at the windscreen.
Cradled in iron,

we steep across the kindled acres.
We salute the fire.

Shadows

In the dream last night, my father
rose from his chair and walked
toward me. How trim he looked,
the weight he carried near the end,
gone. He pointed to water pooling
at the carpet's edge, explained
the necessities of plumbing, how
pipes burst from aging. Even the ceiling
mapped an intricate stain, the rain's
abiding passage. The last time I saw him
he and my mother waved as they
pulled away, car windows down,
late summer, a soft chill: shadows
burning on the underside of morning.

Widow

Twilight is best,
the orange streetlamp
how it turns
each flake to cinder, silence
stitching a cold fire
above the sycamore.

She stands at the open
doorway, watches it
fall, the snow settling out
like a seraph's hem
across the pavement.

She likes to linger there,
inhale its embers —
smell the world aflame
at her doorstep.

Likes the nothingness
of these stars,
ending their lives
at her feet.

What of the sycamore, a soliloquy of branches,
the long casting of its prayer? The sky suffers

in her sooted lung, and what is left? My shadow
roots through the natal weeds, stitched to its

green seam, a sycamore's voltage at my back,
this boreal fuse that drives my body home.

Homing

Each winter I fly back, rest my head
against the latch of trees, old stiles,
a streetlamp I used to know. Each year,
the schoolyard withholds its key.

It happens: I wake one morning,
between selves, neither here
nor there. It happens: this redaction.
The continents in me, shifting.

In the video my father, ten years
younger than I am now, jumps
the privet, grabs and lifts me
endlessly above the fading, yellow grass.

It happens: I turn a street corner,
find myself there, a boy tranced
in the market square. And who knows
which one of us is the apparition.

My Father's Hearing Aid

seems lost without his ear, a silenced spigot,
adrift without a doorway, without
the organ's alluvial crib. For years it was you
I spoke to, my calls transfigured, rendered clear
inside your daily minster, amplified.
It was you who fathered me, lifting my words
into the stirrup of his ear, the body's anvil.
You he reached for each morning, the hour
widening in him then like a canto, birds
hived in the wisteria, their gossip making sense
once more as though it were something
undeniable, unstoppable out there, transfused,
striking the Sistine of his ear.

My Father's Hearing Aid

has taken its place in my mother's ear,
a rectifying machine.

It pleases her with its incoming
lecture of wrens. She smiles,

encounters through my father's ear,
a morning's debris. Theatrical,

costume-like the way she puts in her ear,
another ear. As though

the ear consoles. As though a wren
might put an end to annihilation.

Inch its song inside her, sound as grace.
As though my father is listening

as her body thrums
the motor's unanswerable plea.

Kin

As she gets older the accent of her childhood
returns. I hear it sometimes in the under-song
of her vowels and consonants; that grist and grit
of the Calder region where she grew up, the moor's
hard lines. When my mother moved to London
at seventeen she took elocution lessons to drive
the accent out. I think now she must have hated
that sound, her father's annunciations pinned
inside her own. A relief then, to inhabit new
language, to speak without the fierce gutturals
of that man. But now, I can hear it, the darker
industries of her tongue, that accent creeping back
again like millstone, the earth of her childhood
as she ages, returning; that harness of her kin.

A Story about Childhood

My mother found the dog rooting through
the mulch out back, nosing rotten cabbage leaves,
need pushed deep into its nostrils. What could she
do but love the animal, this famished stray,
dirt steeled firm to its skin. She nursed
the creature round. Took to the fells each day.
Wandered bracken paths high above stacks
and kilns, glad to be absent from the tempers
of that house. It didn't last. Her father kicked
the animal out one night. Snatched his plate
and slammed it at the wall. My mother
rubs her arm as she speaks. Eighty years on,
she still feels it: that sting, that phantom
shard of porcelain.

Searching for My Grandfather

Face it, he offered little in life but the black grit
of his temper, and even that was driven out
of him young, his bones latched quick to sandstone,
shale. My mother was glad to see him gone. Yet
here I am searching the cemetery, walking from plot
to plot as if it matters what I find, as if I can trace
what drove him to become a body of gasoline,
constantly lit and burning. Perhaps it was his father
killed on the first day of the Somme. Losing him
at 15, is that where it began? That first flicker
of carbon? I know where it ends. Some things you
bury deep. My mother did, all his photos, letters,
belongings: ash. Burnt as he once burned everything
around him. Nothing left. Not even a gravestone.

Sundays at My Grandmother's House

By four it was already dusk. The remains of the roast
put away. I'd wander her house then, studying

the walls, the polished brass of stirrups, horseshoes,
yellowed portraits of the dead. All the while

I'd hear her from the next room grumbling at the state
of things, the corner store open now on Sundays.

See her periodically stood by the parlor window
frowning at the young women in their Bombay silks

walking home down Westfield Road. That was 1975.
The mills, factories all but closed. Bradford's skyline

blackening against chimneys, drystone walls. My
grandmother attended her later years, alone. Clayton

Beck flushing its metal through her veins. Her cadence,
hardening. Her face, the silhouette of another world.

Reverie

The rook never sleeps.
It calls from the branches,
the museum of leaves
inside you. Night after
night you climb back,
float up there, observing
the old pastures. Drift
amid the tree's green bell,
listening to your future;
the calculus of rain, a dog
barking, that idle traffic
of wind. Always the same
car passing under you,
announcing its departure.

Hitchhiking at Nineteen

It was always night, starless,
a car now and then, inching past,
its headlights picking out the edges
of pines. Then pitch sky again.
The silhouette of roofs, TV aerials
looming above hedges. The curtained
windows in front of you. That silence
sinking deep. That awful beauty
of standing alone. A streetlamp haloed
above. Always October, its recession
of needles. The dead moving farther
inside you, the past spreading
on the outskirts of towns you'd never
known until now. Your eyes straining
to find the road, its white lines
curving back into moorland, night.

There's the cloud's brumal attic, a flushed sore
clotting beyond the pond's eye. There's the horse

innocent pilgrim, solitary in his oblivion of grasses.
The oak as it opens its ribcage above him. The minus hour,

a fierce subtraction of gales. There's the bell tower
ticking against the mind's delirious pillow.

Crows

convene like angry rectors
in the pulpits of the alder tree.
A dream. A haunting.

A story I tell myself each night
before sleep. To wake then,
breathe that primary air.

Feel once more the timber's root
urging through my skin,
a perpetual divining.

These crows, hour after hour,
arriving in me, their caws
my umbilical key.

Fauré

My father would turn the volume up, lifting
his breakfast spoon at intervals, a kind of conductor

I suppose, the choir beginning to rise in him again
like a flotilla of darkly lit balloons. At least

that's how I remember those mornings, years later,
lost in the mundane labor of another country,

mostly failing at my life. I like to think of him
sat there, consumed by the music building

through the still early hour of that room,
while my mother took to the garden once more,

annoyed no doubt by how loud it had become.
Which is to say, an ordinary morning

in the middle of their lives, where I was a child,
and the house an isle of incalculable light.

Spring Inventory in a Wood Near Lund

The paraffin of bluebells.

The wood, a silent
stove, lit from within.

My father's wood.

His small registry
of delights. All afternoon

the ants spelling their figures
over the needled floor

like hieroglyphs
scattering.

And like my father, I've stood
ankle deep in the brackish
tank of these ferns.

Stretched out in the private
flatbed of my thinking

and studied the circuitry
of alder leaf, branch,

its tidal
constellations.

Sensed in nearby ponds
pikes engage
the trembling arsenal
of their bodies

as I've felt my own skin
quicken to its
suffering,

an inland gull
merely
the pitched cries
of a child, sky
its darkening cradle.

Each spring
I've watched my father
walk deeper
into this wood,

deeper
into its untamed
mansion,

year after year, sleeved
in the clotted weather
of its rooms,

the air's opaque
fractions.

Now this abacus
of stones
turning in my hand

is all I have,

this common
denominator
of trees.

Even so rooks
in the attics
go on delivering
the dusk river
of their songs,

between then and now

all of it spooling
into the evening's

syncopated cavities.

It is late. The wood
a drifting cluster
of inflections

as ants decipher
their paths
along the forest floor
lifting their luggage
once more into the cellars
this earth becomes,

the moon a shilling
burning
at the leaf's green sill

each blade

our porous
oriel.

It is late. The air
another form
of currency.

The bluebells too, a fuel
we know ourselves by

as small as it is, and brief,

mite, wood tick, continuing
their odysseys
through the cemeteries

of branch rot, clay,

the rich kiln,
its lit vocabulary.

Let us speak in this accent
of alder, gull, ant, soil.

Now that you are gone
father,
these words
are all I have.

Helen

Below me, tools insist
    a plain song. Nails enter the hulls
of grounded trawlers —

a pleasant sound,
    the day mending itself again.
I sit above the harbor

and think of the needle
    as it enters you — London flutters
just below your skin.

Another may have thought it
    better to slow-dance
their way down,

one bottle at a time.
    You want it all though —
the sensate charge

pressing its lip on — the faceted light
    that extends like
a Byzantine alley

    through you.

Elegy with Desert Pine and Fennel Seed

for Patrick Lane

I wanted to know the sawmills, the stunted
desert pines. In language, find that hardness,
that way of pushing back. I was young then,
and that hardness made sense. Though it's your
attention to the smaller wardens of the earth —
beetle, spider — that stays with me, your gardens
anodynes, the soils you hunched over each day
listening, farming fennel seeds, burying them
as you'd once buried bottles of vodka — graves
you'd find and empty long after. I'm thinking
of the tiny elephant you carved. That elegance
whittled from a bar of soap. How your patio fed
the calendar of those later years. Hands worn
to the pumice of pine, their hardness earned.

Widower

Barely noon, he parks his cycle at the oak
and passes through the chapel turnstile,

as usual a rucksack slung over his back
heavy with garden tools, a copy of *The Sun*,

wildflowers, lunch. Most days he sits awhile
on the bench nearby, reads a little, then eats.

When done, he walks over and begins routinely
trimming weeds, grasses, circling the perimeter next,

working his spade slowly, digging out a slender
furrow of soil until her grave seems to hover

there almost flawless in its frame. And what else
can he do for her now but this weekly crop

and mend. His beard, face, grown wild.
Below him, daffodils, their ceaseless gold alarms.

My Mother Paints Her First Picture at Ninety

Seams of gray drift silently behind two trees,
stripped, a white lake inching its frostbite

into the canvas. The moon — like her eye —
near perfect in its aperture of grief.

This is how it must be now: the sky
slated against a neutral white, days

without him extending like a fathomless
estate of water. This is what she owns:

the blinding garment of the mere,
her moon, a celestial blister.

In front of her, the infinite manicured grays,
these trees in their soundless blackening,

and a stillness filling her room —
which is starless — sequestered, alone.

Clearing out My Father's Studio

In his last years it had all become too much,
    this mess of inks, watercolors, an inventory

that began to weigh on him, the stuff
    in this room a reminder of what he no longer

practiced, the brushes dry, his calligraphy
    gathering dust in stacks, drawers. As a child,

I'd sit on his lap and watch him work, follow
    the meticulous movement of his pen, watch

as the nib pressed its path into the whiteness
    of the page: an early lesson, precision

a form of prayer. Tonight, packing up paints,
    folios, I'm wading through what stays, what

goes, what I take to remember him as he was;
    a man sat with his son lost in all that making.

The Letter

Between a stack of gray *Observers*, my grandmother's spidery cursive.
How easy it would have been to miss the envelope, to toss it away
with the rest of his collected periodicals, menus, postcards from the churches
he'd visited. Perhaps he thought it a good place to keep it safe, pressed benea
the weight of old news, or maybe he had simply lost track of it. I imagine hin
laid in his bunk, 19 years old, stationed off the coast of Egypt, the war still yo
as he ran his finger along the edge of the envelope. It was six months before
the letter reached his ship. How glad he must have been to receive it, wanting
in that moment to hear of his mother's daily routines. How the weather was
turning warm, his father out back planting the leeks again. It took a page
of local gossip before she could speak it: his sister's passing, and only twelve y
old. Came home with a headache and later that day was gone. All the night r
over London, the doctors supposed. An embolism. I think of him
deep inside the hull, turning away from the other men, the ink starting to blu
in his hand. I look at my grandmother's blotted words. My father's tears
decades dry now, his own life done. These lines worn deep into the grain
of the paper. His thumbprints faint at the edges.

Look past the knuckled hedges, their indices of ice.
Look past the coastal glebes thrashed with hail, paths

treading strange into the shuddering stalls of the outer riding.
Look past the abattoirs, their sulfurs draining

the cavities of noon. Past the frost that latches us
to an hourglass, past our skylines of blackened elm.

Walking to My Father's Grave, I Pass his Old Garden

The trees are gone. Not even a stump left to guide me.
Instead, rows of cabbages, snaps peas, carrots.
Where blossoms once lay, the new owner's trench of leaks.

In later years, the garden was all he knew of the world.
An idle release of a marigold and the apple's journey
toward becoming the hard flesh he picked each morning

and consumed. It's what I'm thinking of today as I pass
the garden, the loam's rich motor. What he gazed at back then
cultivated now by a younger man. But why not make room

for yams, sprouts? I'm on my way with a handful of parsnips.
After all, he had no time for manicured lawns, nor jars of cut
flowers in shops, cemeteries. He preferred the wild clematis,

the spectral wigs of dandelions seeding chapel grounds,
their clocks canceling above the dead.

Visiting D.H Lawrence's Birthplace, Eastwood 1997

I ran my fingers over the chestnut table, your mother's glasses,
her nightdress, that such a thing might remember
the form inside it. Listened for you amid the heirlooms

believing in this room, its quiet furniture, the pull of bed, table,
in this arrangement of things as a way of seeing —
how tiles, curtains, articulated memory, how everything

held still, implicit with life, each chair recalling a figure.
I remember the woman in *Odour of Chrysanthemums*,
of the humble way she dresses her husband's body, feeling

the infinite distance of his skin, how she tidies the kitchen
in a similar fashion, understanding her own mortality
in the permanence of objects, the grace in these things.

How the contents of the room I stood in then
grew redolent, a kind of incantation, charmed.

Surrey Cottage, August 1975

Curtains ajar, air bathing sills,
brass binoculars, an old black iron,
blue bottles knocking fattened
carburetors against panes, walls,
the mantel clock, dogged, fluent
in its two steady bars, inching
between past and present —

silence all the while circulating
in upper more distant rooms,
and always that slow punctuation
of the tap and my father's mother,
seated at the center of it all
in her ancient pinafore, at rest,
like a monarch in shadow.

Assisted Living

for my mother

You've found a rhythm, you tell me,
a way of coping, getting through
your day: morning scripture, lunch,
afternoon walks to the mailbox.

Now that spring is here, it's the wrens
you love, their shallow ticking
over the mulch outside your window,
open once more to the world.

And the hymns you play each night,
lying in the dark before sleep,
imagining the lift and fall of your hands,
the hour fastening in a ligature

of sound. This pattern of surfacing
to the same light, and starlings
at the feeder, you explain, waking you
each morning like children

answering a fierce, habitual greed.

Visiting Adelstrop with My Mother

Nothing left but a bench,
the repainted platform sign.

Rail tracks long removed,
refunded to the earth.

We sit, wait. A crown of gnats
feeding at our ankles.

Everywhere the sweet punk
of parsley, blackthorn. Rosehips

in the hedges, their tumors,
fattening. My father gone

a year now. A lone skylark
wavers in the blue allotments

above us, its body, song,
farming an inscrutable air.

Maestro

His hair burned silver
at the root, shone
in the scissor-edges —

those steel birdsongs
his fingers scored,
hovering at our scalps.

How carefully then
he broomed what we'd
given up into the bins

of late afternoon. Our
hair newly cropped,
our ears, denuded sails

steering us through
the metals of winter.

Night Fishing as a Boy

Wind troubles the surface of the pond,
a station of reeds on the opposite shore

gathering dark in their blades. I breathe
into the vessel of my hands, keep an eye

on the silver bobber, wait for contractions
of the line. How old am I in this dream?

Perhaps it's my father huddled at banks' edge —
not me — his hands gripping the nylon rod,

crouched under the trees' bare awning.
Perhaps it's the winter of 1933, a fleet of

sparrows flooding dogwoods above the mere
as my father waits in that dusk for carp

to hook, night, line, all of it unravelling
beneath the moon's splintered marquee.

Landscape with Father and Son

My son jambs stone after stone into shale, forges
a miniature henge as wind slams its wrecking-ball

from the North. Little's changed; sky retains a gray
exterior, surf dragging pebbles, jellies, bladder-

wrack across open shore. When I look seaward,
or down, our worlds appear the same, both of us

digging into damp shelled sand. And kneeling here,
backs to the Marine Hotel, carpark, town, how easy

to imagine my father is still alive, sat in his car
behind us, belly full of cod, chips, trying to doze

now while watching our hands — as he'd once
watched mine — build rock by rock a ragged folly,

wind pummeling hard at the chassis, refusing —
as it always did — his body, his mind, their sleep.

Self Portrait as a Lighthouse

Easy to find correlatives.
You know the derelict cafe

is the wind's asylum.
That deserted bench,

the sum of poverty.
You inhabit the verges

of this song, neck-deep
amid the salt-scrim,

a pummeled scar,
storm-wrecked, sheer

above the Atlantic's steel
horizon. Each night,

mind ablaze, you plow
the gale's blind acre.

Roadkill

An eye closed, not in death
perhaps but in concentration,

or sleep, an ear tuned
to the sunless custodians

laboring under him.
I'm trying to make a poem

of things again. My daughter
asleep at last in her seat

behind me, the engine working
its refrain. Let morning be

what it is: a stubborn frost,
this animal busted

on the asphalt, its body
in my rear-view, insistent,

clear.

Elegy with the Lark Ascending

If there is a theme here, let it be this:
Williams' *The Lark Ascending*, my father
asleep as the heat settles over
his slippers, over the stilled acre
of his dreaming, his books initialing
the unlit passage home. Let it be
the chapel bell, its iron another detail
inside the instrument of silence.
Let it be my mother humming above
the vegetables, stove-blushed, stirring
the liver in, her spoon a tiny piston
inside this poem, turning over root
and organ. Let it be this soundtrack
of pearl churring at the glass,
the minutes loosening hand upon them.
The gardens abandoned tonight,
each one, solitary, agitated, prone.

Notes

Spurn Point is a narrow peninsula that curves between the North Sea and the Humber Estuary. The peninsula was last breached during a storm in 2013.

"Reading Edward Thomas to My Father" includes phrases from Thomas's poem "Adelstrop."

The poem "On the Platform of Paragon Station" references the statue of Philip Larkin by sculptor Martin Jennings.

"After the Call from the Night Nurse" references Vincent van Gogh's last painting *Wheatfield with Crows.*

"Nocturne" includes the phrase, "localized deafness" by Roland Barthes from his book *Mourning Diary.*

The poem "Sundays at My Grandmother's House" references Clayton Beck, a source river for Bradford Beck, which runs through the city center of Bradford, West Yorkshire.

"Elegy with Desert Pine and Fennel Seed" is for the Canadian poet Patrick Lane, who grew up and lived for much of his life in British Columbia.

"Elegy with a Lark Ascending" includes in its title Ralph Vaughan Williams' 1914 violin and piano composition, "The Lark Ascending."

The Author

Adam Chiles was born in London and grew up in East Yorkshire, England. He is the author of a previous collection, *Eveningland*, nominated for the 2009 Gerald Lampert Award. His work has appeared in *Copper Nickel*, *Gulf Coast*, *Indiana Review*, *Threepenny Review*, *Willow Springs*, and elsewhere. Adam lives with his wife Emily and their children in rural Virginia.

www.ingramcontent.com/pod-product-compliance
Lightning Source LLC
Chambersburg PA
CBHW020612310726
48979CB00008B/1446/J

* 9 7 8 1 9 3 9 5 7 4 3 7 4 *